Gas Chamber

ALSO BY AHMAD AL-KHATAT

The Bleeding Heart Poet
Love on the War's Frontline
Wounds from Iraq
Roofs of Dreams

Gas Chamber

poems by
Ahmad Al-Khatat

Poetic Justice Books
Port St. Lucie, Florida

©2019 Ahmad Al-Khatat

book design and layout: SpiNDec, Port Saint Lucie, FL
cover image: *Sacrificial Poppies*, ©2018 Kris Haggblom

All rights reserved.

No part of this book may be used or reproduced in any manner whatsoever without written permission except in the case of brief quotations embodied in critical articles and reviews. Members of educational institutions and organizations wishing to photocopy any of the work for classroom use, or authors, artists and publishers who would like to obtain permission for any material in the work, should contact the publisher.

Published by Poetic Justice Books
Port Saint Lucie, Florida
www.poeticjusticebooks.com

ISBN: 978-1-950433-32-2

SECOND EDITION
10 9 8 7 6 5 4 3 2

dedication

*I would like to present this writing to my family
for giving me all the inspiration
and support I need
mainly, my beautiful princess Noemi Stafford*

contents

forward by Patricia Ann Mayorga   ix

Damaged	3
Gas Chamber	4
Goodbye Friend	5
Is It Too Late to Apologize	6
Dance on the Lines	8
My Son Traveled	10
Dear Grief	11
My Neck Is Ready	13
Death Grew Within Me	14
Mr. Bullet	16
The Scent of the Grave	18
Sing My Depression	20
Life or Death	22
Chess Game	24
Handsome Guest	25
Men with Makeup	27
Thank You, Selfie	29
One Woman	30
Life of a Student	32
My Grief Over Thirty Years	33
English Is My Second Language	34
Depressed from This World	35
Good Morning	36
City of Joys	37
Ugly Reality of My World	38
The Time Traveler	39
The Rainbow Saved My Life	40
Tears of the Moon	41

The Music of Life's Pleasure	42
Museum of Corpses	43
Money Buys Happiness	45
My Collections Over the Years	46
If My Name Were Baghdad	48
Four Cigarettes and Two Ice Cream	49
In Darkness Alone	51
Along	52
Veil of the Moon	53
Blood and Ashes	54
I Am the Water...	55
We Are Lost	56
Tears Fall from My Eyes	58
I Yearn for You	60
A Dark Soul in a Healthy Church	61
The Demon of My Religion	64
I Witnessed My Death	68

Forward

I first met Ahmad Al-Khatat through his submission to *Poets' Espresso Review* in October of 2018. Reading his submissions, I immediately realized that this young poet was haunted by the horrors of war and, through his words, it was evident that Ahmad carried the burden of his early beginnings in his heart and soul. And what other way to move through that darkness, than through the expression of poetry. Born May of 1989, Ahmad lived in Iraq with his family until the age of five after the regime of Saddam Hussein. Feeling hopeless, the family sought refuge in Syria but suffered poor treatment as so many discriminated against Iraqi people often blaming them for the wars that had riddled the Middle East for years. Ahmad and his family lived in Syria until his tenth year when they immigrated to Montreal, Canada, where he now lives.

Recently, Ahmad made the decision to visit his homeland of Iraq which was his first visit since his family fled in 1994. This trip would impact Ahmad in a way he had not expected. As a child, his confusion of his identity of being Iraqi was immense. Only remembering a country of war, he did not know what to expect upon his visit to Iraq and would find the experience as one of enlightenment. Not only would he visit beautiful sites and monuments of restoration of a country, his homeland, that has existed under the influence of endless war,

Ahmad Al-Khatat

but he would reflect on the suffering, death, and destruction that somehow has engrained itself as a seed in this prolific poet. Internalizing the immensity of his roots born from a country of continuous conflict, Ahmad sees death, even his own, as one of confusion but shared with me that when his time comes to meet death, he will walk up to him, a stoic remnant that survived when many of his fellow Iraqi people did not.

Currently, Ahmad studies religion at Concordia University in Montreal, Canada; however, his passion is history. He is driven to study, learn and understand the historical events that have shaped the world today. In the meanwhile, the following pages filled with Ahmad's poetry, emanates his passion to see the goodness in life where his words emerge from the depths of the dark side of mankind yet seeks to find the light and goodness in our common humanity.

— Patricia Ann Mayorga, Editor-in-Chief, *Poets' Espresso Review*, United States of America

Gas Chamber

Ahmad Al-Khatat

Damaged

Everything in my life is damaged
the flames of the day are damaged
and dust of darkness is damaged
peace damages and causes wars
wars damage and causes peace
kids damaged and run from tanks
schools in my village are damaged
teachers cry with damaged chalks
students yearn for damaged blackboards
the sightless bones are damage
the deaf beings are damaged too
the mute politicians are the last damaged
the father repairs the damaged door
the mother prays next to the damaged windows
out of the blue, their son arrives in a damaged coffin

Ahmad Al-Khatat

Gas Chamber

My life lately seems like a gas chamber,
everything appears in different colours nowadays
my name is no longer important since I've got
a number and soon I will have a legal price tag
I thought the snow would cover the cruelty of blood suckers
yet, I saw a broken cage in spring with blood and
feathers of the love birds above the winter rain
with no tweets to welcome the depressed autumn
the sun shines at midnight and it looks as if the
city is on fire, with flames around my glowing path
so many times, and nobody is bright to reveal the
sun before death starts collecting my soul
I have been blinded as I wish to go back to
the days where my sight always smiled and never
cried for watching my old pictures of memories
with tears falling in silence of my depression

Goodbye Friend

Why did you leave me without saying goodbye friend?
Weren't we friends, even though you were sick?
Weren't you my teacher in poetry and rhythms?

A joyous attack on my spirit whenever I heard you,
Emotional tears drop of a bird singing your songs.
With faith I pray for you, to see you in heaven.

I walk and I physically feel sick and very cold,
Seeking for a scent, looking for two crying eyes.
So, I embrace your soul and sleep next to you.

I call you many times, and nobody answers.
I miss you everyday, and I still dream of you alone.
The night can't be a night, if I breathe by myself.

I grabbed a red grape from the old giant tree.
The branches wept of my grief for missing you.
I dropped winery tears, and I stayed sadly drunk.

I blindly walk with a cane, I live with no dreams.
You have gone far away, I am thirsty to see you.
Goodbye friend, we will be crying in Baghdad again.

Ahmad Al-Khatat

Is It Too Late to Apologize

I look at the moon with all the hanging stars,
It's minutes away from reaching dawn.

Will this page hold my sorrows with my ink,
Since nobody spent time hearing my words?

Is it too late to apologize to all of my friends,
I have been lying to all, by being a caring one?

Baghdad you are the motherland of my coffin,
will you offer me a grave to dig my whole flesh?

Nobody should weep for reading my apologies,
It does explain why I don't have a loyal shadow.

You loved me more than I loved my broken heart,
I don't hate anybody but I miss your love the most.

The eyes have finished dropping more sorrows,
The lips have dried of flirting with all beautiful ladies.

Alone the spirit stayed hopeful, looking for a way
To force me going to swim in the river where we met.

So, I come out wet without grief for living in misery,
But the moon saw me talking about you to the stars.

I talked about how beautiful it is to have loyal friends,
Who won't stab you in your chest and back at once.

Gas Chamber

I asked God to relieve the breathing with depression,
He told me, help yourself first and I will help you gently.

I asked death how many days I am away from the end,
He answered me, I will be the last Iraqi bleeding to death.

I asked my grandpa for a way to be happy and humble,
He cried and said, how can you be happy when you are blind?

I asked you to come back in a dream for a few minutes,
You walked away because you were no different from them.

Is it too late to apologize; to kiss the sharp knife before
I feel the cold metal cutting my arteries in an extreme way?

Ahmad Al-Khatat

Dance on the Lines

Yesterday I was thinking about two things,
One was you and second was a sad poem.

You once closed my eyes and kissed my dry
Lips who haven't played with tongues forever.

I opened my eyes with a great feeling and
A smile shut my concerns temporarily off.

You were known as a great ballerina,
Who I would enjoy watching a piece of.

Once I took my old tired notebook and
A black pen to write a random poem.

Truly I was looking at your positions of
Your moves and an image I took of you

On one line paper of a notebook I decided
To allow you to dance on the lines by yourself.

To change I tried to define why my poems
Were sad, depressing and heart breaking.

With your positions of ballet, you corrected
My deep writing in the dark of sedans.

And defined why my tears can't ever see in
People, perhaps you always wipe it away from me.

Gas Chamber

No fears needed, you just watch a bit from
My sharp black pen which might kill you by accident.

Change my sorrowful tears into a joyful tear,
Change comes back to stay in between my arms.

Out of sadness I see my happy words that didn't
Change into happy words to end my poem.

I looked for you and couldn't find you anywhere
And realized my black pen started writing a mixture

Of blood red and black to watch you throw
Away on the bottom page bleeding and stabbing

Your back with my black pen when he wrote it
The date of the day of where the poem was writing.

I started crying as a kid who broke his finger,
With my heart who felt full of aches everywhere.

And realized why my poems have a taste of
Bitter endings because her blood is all over

My notebooks which makes it harder for me
To write a happy one after I killed my happiness.

Ahmad Al-Khatat

My Son Traveled

My son traveled before
death recognized his
early bird arrival

the war is over and
he hated me because I
welcomed him in a coffin

My dreams about
him were colourful
Now they are sorrows

only if he knew
my tears have
his scent of him in

Heaven …

Dear Grief

Dear grief
It's been a while
Since we have been crying
For the same reasons

Will I still be alive?
To meet with joy
That I missed years ago
Cause of my depression?

I just want a new touch
In the bosom of the dawn
With sweet lips to kiss
That I feel tirelessly for once

My freedom is dusty
And my passion is weak
I cannot wait to stop
Boiling my jealousy more

New pages are moist
From witnessing me crying
Being lonesome is like a jail
Without a lock to unlock it

I have been honest to all
Like the sea mirror to the moon
They all became the sea waves
When I was the sand castle

Ahmad Al-Khatat

There is always a second chance
And time to forgive and forget
But people judge once and
Decide carelessly to die

My hands write to the lovers
Lovers who hate my words
Words can't describe how much
Love I have for a beautiful lady

Dear grief, I will wait for you
To share with you my new life
So you can remember
The reasons why I still love you

Gas Chamber

My Neck Is Ready

My neck is ready
To be slaughtered by your knife
I deserve absolutely nothing
From this funny life and its lies

I lived in exile and my breath
In alcohol and nicotine for cancer
I pour tears and I did bleed
For friends who are now being evil

I survived comments said by haters
Judging my life due to my skin color
I fought for my right as a good citizen
To the point where I see nothing but death

Life is too short to overthink about hope
When the person made me the happiest
Lied to me and stabbed me with a smile
Time is running like a kiss that tastes betrayal

I love people when they shut their doors
And leave me outside singing like a fool
I hate everyone who cares about my days
When I was just thinking about dying in darkness

Should I write more when nobody supports me?
They all went on highways to the sun of success
When I am still waiting for inspiration to arrive
Therefore, I could find a reason why shall I live longer

Under the raining clouds of autumn leaves
I walked and became a cloud of my misery
I squeezed myself in tears of over thinking about
The positive and negative thoughts about our love.

Ahmad Al-Khatat

Death Grew Within Me

From the day destiny
Chose life for my spirit
And a sad death to your soul

Therefore, I hated life
I grew death within me
And made a wish to die young

I started growing
Sorrows from the past
Crying and making tears weep

I lost so much joy
While I seek for hope
To light myself into a new candle

Friends laughed and said
Stop being so mean to yourself
While I am bleeding their trust away

I walked in the dark mornings
To hear the sea waves misery tells
I knew everyone betrayed nowadays

The woman I loved before was
She? A suffering dream to become
A true or was it my fantasies to hate myself

Gas Chamber

A true lover can be described
Flowers spoke to me about everything
Then why didn't you break my heart beats?

Shall I say that now life is a good?
I met you and your eyes hide our family
I am worried about who will be missed first

The train of death wishes is nearby
Stop me from getting in the dark dawn
If not, then let me rest between your hands

Close my eyes, kiss me like doves do
Just tell me why should I ask the sun to shine
While you are still under the fall clouds

Ahmad Al-Khatat

Mr. Bullet

Mr. bullet comes and hits
The bone inside of my life

Let me die like a volcano
Vomiting all the blood I own

I am not a mistake
Nor a criminal, but only a poet

I deserve death more
Then a bird asking for grains

The water runs down
But my mistakes, they go higher

I write an ink of Baghdad
I died many times with dry tears

Lack of hope building up
Forget about my friend's funerals

My mother once told me that
Grievings are pointless to be recalled

I wish if she knew that my sorrows
Hold a strong coffin I have made

So I could welcome death fearlessly
And die and raise my blood to the moon

Gas Chamber

Therefore, my beloved, forgives me
And pulls the trigger to shoot me down

While I am drunk and smoking a cigar
Unable to defend my mind or my heart

Kill me now or kiss my lips before
I cut my tongue out and die pricelessly

Ahmad Al-Khatat

The Scent of the Grave

When I was a child, I was only able to smell the
 roses of spring.
As I was growing up, my two eyes were silently
 dropping tears.

Before I learnt that they were under the heart of
 the darkness,
For feeling guilty, for not shaking their hands
 days ahead.

I saw a white dove, singing my dead grandma's
 favourite love song,
Trying to make my father happy, and breathe out of
 his depression.

I smelled a longing from the white dove wings,
 watching my father
Holding old photo albums, moaning, laughing, crying
 and smiling.

The martyrs smelled of death years ago, and yet
 he welcomed
Him with a big heart, knowing that he won't be
 honoured to heaven.

Where he would create a cloud, that drop of warm
 rain that grew
More red roses, with the scent of the grave,
 reminding his family.

Gas Chamber

I asked death, why do we stop weeping after awhile, he answered
Me, cause you smell of their scent and their gravesite, bringing joy.

Therefore, do not be confused if you ever see your beloved washing
Her beautiful face of the scent of the dust above your future shrine.

Since is only available in between your hands, and above your tomb.
Which is way all the visitors feel deeply confident, like a newborn angel.

Visiting their missing ones, which is the last purest home to all souls,
And remember, they are always trying hard to make you happier than others.

Ahmad Al-Khatat

Sing My Depression

I want to sing
My depression loud
By the nightingale
Not in a concert
Or school theatre

I prefer to sing in
The streets of
the City of love
By heart breakers
On the sidewalks

By the orders
Of failures like me
When my writings
Were pointless too
Read to the blindfolded

I will sing till
My veins dry out
Of bleeding and
Drink my tears
Within a poison

This is life
Over awhile ago
I now have no
Dreams or hopes
For me anymore

Gas Chamber

Always drunk
Always sinner
Always anxiety
Always sleepless
Shut me down.

I will sing
By neighbors' doors
That won't open
Even if I try
By miserable windows

Baghdad has enough
Sorrows and tears
My story is
Days and nights
Of moving grief.

Ahmad Al-Khatat

Life or Death

My spirit has
Asked me questions,
Like a musician
Playing melancholy flute

Life or death?
Wilder wounds always extend
Hope or fortune?
Burning tears and not fallen

Skeleton or flesh?
Autumn cloud raining blood
Hard or warm hearted?
Heartbroken to be heartless

Mirror or shades?
The wind of late hours
Morning or dawn?
Twilight on the dull road

Cure or luck?
The sorrow of demons
Nightingale or nightmare?
Hidden dream of the future

Vampire or empire?
Slaughter sword in the graveyard
Figurine or fame?
The dictator forgives and never forgets

Gas Chamber

Ink or a notepad?
Thoughts that can be judged by God
Sickness or inspiration?
A misery blooming in a colourless rose

Whispers or tears?
Echo of a lost spirit in Baghdad
Hunter or ghost?
Enemy who hates himself mostly

Party or funeral?
Holiday with a bloody screaming
Nest or mysteries?
Burning candle celebrating my loneliness

Ahmad Al-Khatat

Chess Game

I played chess against my low self-esteem,
My pawns did not move by my directions,
Instead, they all communicated in self-murder.

The rocks were strong;
I burned them all on a bonfire of no regrets,
Because I only wanted my heart to be the rock.

The knights were running;
I gave him emotional letters of yearnings,
They died of thirst and flowed to heaven.

The bishops were weeping;
When I walked by the little king room you made,
And I talked to your roses in the dusty vase.

I had one queen, but she died a while ago,
She was the joy from my smile, and she was
The hopes and dreams I wanted to do for her.

And I am the king in a chase game alone like
A fool playing with nobody but moving two
Teams whenever I don't want to feel lonely.

I love my queen and if she ever comes by
Tell her that I am still waiting to play to
Lose the game but ready to cuddle again.

Gas Chamber

Handsome Guest

I can't heal
My broken heart,
If I crush
My confident wings.

Therefore,
I met a friend,
Or, should I
Say handsome guest.

No words
Were spoken aloud,
No emotions
Were even readable.

Then, I knew
It was death.
He wore a suit
Sewed with miserable colors.

He spoke with
A language of regret,
He can't even smile
Nor, weep a single tear.

I told him
That I waited for today,
And I wished
to die in the moment.

Ahmad Al-Khatat

He wrote me
Let God love you,
And stop avoiding
The blessings of life.

I wrote him
How about my pain,
Why can't I
Find the happy path.

He started bleeding,
I was breaking my muscles.
He cried miserably
When I was drinking his blood.

I wept as well
To smell my childhood,
I did not die but
I forgave death for life.

Men with Makeup

I once remember
Playing with my
Sister's dolls and
My mother's makeup.

They were pure
And honest to
Make a clown's
Face to laugh.

Nothing like me
I breathe with
The strangers' mask
In my journey.

I put one
Two and three,
I seem powerful
From the mind.

I wipe my
Four five
Six and I feel
Weaker and weaker.

Wearing them all
Creates confusion
To tell myself
That it's alright.

Ahmad Al-Khatat

Those masks were
Men's makeup that
Hid sadness and
Tears of hopes.

Death told me;
You won't find
A mask anymore
On my death day.

My dreams died;
My tears dried;
My old makeup
Damaged my life.

Can't
Wipe the past,
Can't
Heal the present,
Till I die joyfully.

Gas Chamber

Thank You, Selfie

Thank you, selfie, for shooting untruthful images,
My friends see my smiles and they judge blindly,
Not realizing that most of my pictures are cloudy,
With tears appearing in pictures by myself.

People ask me questions one after another,
More than wishing or answering my questions,
I can't blame them anymore since today, society
Is growing liars into leaders and ignoring others.

Sometimes I find myself talking to nails,
The mirror doesn't feel my sorrow's rhymes,
The picture frames are painful to be hung
On the dull wall that makes me want to die.

I took selfies and lied to everyone,
Before pulling the trigger to shoot myself,
I could stab myself but it's not as satisfying
As cold metal touches flesh and blood drips

The birds fly but I can't fly with them,
Because I grow with my parents' grief
My mind and heart could never sleep,
As a blind man is a poet of his pain and death.

Ahmad Al-Khatat

One Woman

Under the darkness of the night
In between the smoke of my cigar
Next to the half empty cup of wine
I was laying down on my rusty bed

Apologizing to my innocent spirit
I started torturing slowly and slowly
With tears burning my faith harshly
No sounds, my heart was moaning

So much dark was getting outside
Like my Baghdad, with more grief
It seemed the birth of the depression
My flesh started missing the scent of tomb

I smiled like an orphan dreams to have wings
I laughed like a homeless person dreams to stand up
I cried like a prisoner dreams to be one politician
I regretted to light on the candle of more sorrows

The dawn came and nobody felt of my pain
A perfume from the distance of the moon
Came upon my body, and stopped everything
Her touches relieve my aches for the moments

Gas Chamber

It was the woman who melted the paradise
With her black robe and she seemed like a star
I have been fearless of the nights and mornings
I became a sinner of kissing and cuddling her

One man can easily lose his own value
But with a woman life seems much better
With her hands you won't be in the graveyard
Until, your jealous brain stops your loving heart

Ahmad Al-Khatat

Life of a Student

Being a student, is no different
from the life of a prisoner, waiting
on his pardon or walking barefoot
toward the bloody cord of death
I chose what I wanted to study for
more than one sleepless night
I lose count on my hours of sleep
As my sweet dreams fade away
the teacher becomes ruthless
with unclear homework, and exams
studying past midnight, it hurts me deep.
I am in a nightmare of endless deadlines
with my tears I write him a letter
asking him to pass me with an average
Instead he ignores me and enjoys
watching me suffer in his classroom again
while I hide my bruises under
my eyes I received from my abusive
classmates, I hide my suicidal cuts
on my arms with long sleeve shirts

My Grief Over Thirty Years

Since I was born in a foreign country
a kind of grief broke my heart into tales
that would heal your soul, and burn my friendship away
When I was five years old, grief started
a journey with me, finding the dark truth,
and meeting friends from rich families who
think about owning the stairs to heaven
When I was ten years old, grief took me
to a higher level of realistic depression and
blew me as an autumn leaf to the North Pole
where I realized that my end is much closer
When I was twenty years old, grief changed
my faith to a lost soul and muscles into fat
inside my mind, I started sadly surviving
from diaries I had written when I was drunk
When I was twenty-five years, grief tore me
apart and folded my breath away from the untold
stories, even my mother made me feel that
I am the unwanted son of the family I love the most
When I will turn thirty years old, I will wake up alone
with grief to the scent of innocent childhood
memories, tears will fall as much as the sips
of alcohol are damaging my life's lungs and kidneys

Ahmad Al-Khatat

English Is My Second Language

English is my second language
I cross miles and miles away
from my religion, I accept the
fact I am a refugee
with a broken heart
I am now the monster
from a different culture
I go to the mosque, as my enemies
call me a terrorist however their
parents are the cause of why I am
here in grief, from dawn to dusk
I go to church as a stranger
as the believers judge me as racist
as if Jesus was not meant for all mankind
I am a sinner, as I walk back home
I learned how to defend myself
by taking courses in a public school
to complete people's judgemental
thoughts about me, as I die as wolf
trapped in a cage, called society
in media I am a soul hooked on the
wall of the sky but in reality, I was
an innocent man merged in the clouds

Gas Chamber

Depressed from This World

I have recently put my mind for sale,
If you are curious to understand why
It is nothing personal or harmful but
I am just depressed from this world
I observe the tree breaking its own
branches and blowing the leaves away.
I tried to read the drifting leaves as I knew
it was a sign of my grief and sorrow
Love is a mix tape, playing in my head,
As it hurts since I am too weak to understand,
I listen to one song at a time while my
neighbour is digging a hole to pull the trigger
My decisions about my marriage are
more than a thousand miles away from
my miserable reality, compared to a
death I am closer to rather than happiness
Those ordinary people have lost their
Colours and thoughts as my mind is
being thrown away only because it has
a piece of pie for all the dying children.

Ahmad Al-Khatat

Good Morning

I wake up on my alarm clock,
It doesn't say to me good morning
I drink my first cup of coffee,
It doesn't say to me good morning
I eat my first bites of bacon,
It doesn't say to me good morning
I see my same old neighbour,
he doesn't say to me good morning
I take the bus to go to work
Nobody says to me good morning
I arrive at work, my coworkers
and customers don't say good morning
I am so lonely that I forget to say
to the photos in my office good morning

Gas Chamber

City of Joys

My days are like dry leaves,
they are everywhere and
always in the corners of
Sorrowful streets, in the city of joys
Every love story dies in my dreams,
people are more hurtful than before
And the night is longer than what they say
life is short so drink until you fall asleep
Nowadays my eyes wish to be blind
like the candle that celebrates marriages
and funerals, the sky watches and apologizes to
the clouds and rain, waiting until my eyes stop
weeping
I will never understand how to smile
by the broken branches and dead trees,
my happiness will come back to me
after I drown my laughing face to death

Ahmad Al-Khatat

Ugly Reality of My World

I did not choses to be a poet
nor a man with a mind that
cannot understand all the
questions that life demands
endlessly and mercilessly, I hardly
hear the echoes of tomorrow
the man that walks with a cane is a
hero that crosses over into a dirty town
to the corner of the damaged street
to feed what humans have stepped
over more once, when it was a bleeding
hand asking for words of mercy
young and healthy brains are
always in coffeeshops and libraries
able to spend hours and days
trying to figure out how the rainbow
comes after a depressing moment
after it was rains, like blind prayers
my grandpa was always up early
going out with a dog for a small walk
holding tight onto the leash as if it was
the only thing that kept him alive
until the day he released the dog and
instead caught the newspaper and read
about my uncle's death in the war
that should never be in spring,
since the enemies have destroyed
all roses and flowers, but lost
from spreading the rise of death
that will lead to a bloody revenge

Gas Chamber

The Time Traveller

If I had a time machine
I would not go the dark part
that built me up sad;
or ahead to my unknown
destiny and fearful future
I would take it and go with it
to the cemetery to bring me back
to the last moments of my friends
and see what the solution could be
instead of staring at their photos
I would then walk to my parents with it
and see if they could fix what they
damaged for myself and my siblings,
As I still hate the way they taught me
how to cry, far away from the tomb of my homeland
to this day, I feel I have been adopted
to a woman who she deeply loves me
meanwhile, I always look for a hammer
a few nails, to hook my dreams above
the broken bridge, with a prayer from my falling tears

Ahmad Al-Khatat

The Rainbow Saved My Life

The last rainbow that appeared,
recognized me from my eyes
he told me that I survived the war
and that he saved my life
he said that back in my homeland
he can't be seen when he appears,
instead he helps the angels to paint by
Marking the children with my colours
he painted red on the ones that died
he painted orange on the hungry ones
he painted yellow on the ill ones
he painted green on the orphaned ones
he painted blue on the heavily wounded ones
he painted indigo on the ones with last breath
and lastly, he painted me with violet
to live between all of my old friends
Whom died, and I did not

Gas Chamber

Tears of The Moon

What have we done,
our lives are in danger
everywhere we go it is
More cloudy in autumn
we die like summer flies
Children play 'til death separates them
like a grandfather with a backache
working over hours without a cane
my hands do what my mind
doesn't want, I don't know
who I should talk with, my
loud enemies or voiceless tombs
my house is now owned by a
stranger, as he dreams to stab my
flesh to release his anger from
the days of the ignorant war we had
today, blood is the colour of victory
even black is the colour to celebrate
a death of a dear friend and not his birthday
since mothers are widows and orphans
you read or either hear my words
wondering if I will be drinking or
crying like the time when I lost all my
hopes and dreams from this world
I will be a solider fighting with ink
That could be the cause of my death
since some faces find a grave is better
knowledge than being awake from tears of the moon

Ahmad Al-Khatat

The Music of Life's Pleasure

Friday night, I was
walking around in the
middle of the city, where
the murders are realistic
my brain has been burned
from everyone who enjoys all
the sights unseen and are drunk
from the wealthy wolves' intentions
one woman ran into me
with a sweaty face and ripping off
clothes, asking me if I saw her best
friend before she lost her bride's dress
another man who was bare with
a hundred tattoos, piercings
and a thousand cuts from drugs
asked me if the music of life's pleasure was over

Gas Chamber

Museum of Corpses

Inside
museum
of corpses
there are
dead refugees
bodies who
died 'cause
they were
not characters,
but priceless,
experiments
That helped
humankind,
with plastic
surgery, they
test dangers
And feature
The weapons
Of flesh
and blood,
crash test
dummies,
design body
armour against
the aliens
from the
spaceship
and women,
private body

Ahmad Al-Khatat

parts were
all set
to put on
sale, since
all the
hairstylists
and
cosmetics
had been
working
hard to
keep their
belief in
Death.
It does not
have to
be boring
inside the
mind of
Lively souls

Money Buys Happiness

Tomorrow, I will sell
my tears, smiles, and sweats
to buy stationery for back
to school to my little boy
After tomorrow, I will sell
my heart, mind, and wellness
to buy school uniform and
books to my little daughter
On the weekend, I will sell
my emotions, secrets, and feelings
to release my teenager, boy
from the prison for dealing with drugs
Next unknown month, I will sell
my eyes, tongue, and two ears
to stop my adult daughter from
creating more reasons to say goodbye
After another sad year, I will sell
my dusty flesh, rusty bones, and faith
to finally myself a grave with a
tomb written on it "money buys happiness"

Ahmad Al-Khatat

My Collections Over the Years...

When I was eight, I started collecting
Ants in a small box. I ate the crazy
Ones and kill the rest, for no reason

When I was ten, I started collecting
Spiders killing them right away and
destroyed their webs, for no reason

When I was twelve, I started collecting
Bugs and flies. I broke their wings
And watched them dying, for no reason

When I was fourteen, I started collecting
Autumn leaves to hide the dead animals
From the busy streets, for no reason

When I was sixteen, I started collecting
Lost words and tied them into free verses
I wore them over my neck, for no reason

When I was eighteen, I started collecting
Birds feathers to write from the ink of my tears
For Letters to my dead friends, for no reason

When I was twenty one, I started collecting
Numbers on my old phone. I never called a
lady from the club I went before, for no reason

<u>Gas Chamber</u>

When I was twenty four, I started collecting
Empty bottles of women scent, to smell
Them and pretend to be in love, for no reason

When I was twenty six, I started collecting
Empty cans of soda and other cheap beers
I gave them to the homeless, for no reason

When I am twenty nine, I started not to
Collect anything, only because I knew that
My homeland has no more space for my death.

Ahmad Al-Khatat

If My Name Were Baghdad

If my name were Baghdad
I wouldn't to be a soldier
I'd rather be Frankenstein
To kill the death planner and
save the kids to play happily

If my name were Baghdad
I'd fly with angel wings
spreading love and peace
only so nobody would cry
as much as I do every night

If my name were Baghdad
I'd create a route away from
Fear of my yearnings, and
my dreams to create hope to
walk barefoot in my village

If my name were Baghdad
I'd break down the boundaries
and bury the war weapons
that caused the blindness to
dream far from my two hands

If my name were Baghdad
I will add more diamonds by
the shining stars and knock
on the door of the cemetery
To visit the spirits of the heroes

Gas Chamber

Four Cigarettes and Two Ice Cream

Today the summer breeze was frozen
And the sun was raining more heat
It felt as if the earth is browsing the
Climate of sinners, and not heaven

I went out and decide to visit my friend
So many laughs, so many drinks I had
Although, I was not happy from the inside
I had to ask him for a cigarette to smoke

He refused and I cried from the inside
But my ego forced me to take one, two,
Three, and four. Meanwhile he stopped
Drinking and he told me "you are not alone"

I believe he thought I am rushing to
Say goodbye from this miserable life
Perhaps, I am drinking my poison as
Gently as I can, waiting for the sign

I left from my friend house sad and
Feelings lonesome again and this
Time was worse than before only
My heart was aching to stop beating

I saw my brother and he bought
Me two ice creams to feel cooler
I ate them and started talking to
Him, and I wanted to die with no

Ahmad Al-Khatat

Worries whether I will go to
Heel alone, or suffer more with
Tears burnings my flesh 'till
My wounds turn into bleeding cuts

Four cigarettes and two ice creams
They did not stop me from crossing the
Lines of society rules only to save
The rainbow for a lifetime and sentence

Myself for a unknown judgments
Waiting to lose my sight to forget
The faces and their plans from
Lying and never stabbing to death

Gas Chamber

In Darkness Alone...

First face death then live in the glory of life

It's not hard to know where the heart lives

From a cigarette, up in smoke misery arose

Dreams are no longer good as gold as before

Standing in the rainbow, with eyes still raining

My friend says do not stay up late with a bottle

Meanwhile, I am just keeping myself calm in dark

Finding motherland, is like the death in my shadow

Deep in my wounds, I heard that sad song years ago

Nothing good about being drunk in darkness alone

Ahmad Al-Khatat

Along

I lay down on my bed at late midnight
Unfortunately, I cannot rest like some do
However, I rethink about everything I
Said or did to a friend, or even to a stranger

The night is silent but not my thoughtful
Brain, and mouth with my voiceless vows
I feel I am in a deathbed with no cares from
Anyone I know, but with my friendly shadows

My life will never tell me the story to its end
Hard to be up along the night, with watery eyes
Revelation is a lie that all languages define
As one hero is drowning in the sea of ambition

Along the night and before I fall asleep
No more smiles worth to express my love
More of sorrows needed be to explained to nobody
When most of us, we forget about the good actions

Gas Chamber

Veil of the Moon

My heart has many doors for you tonight
Many candles I have for our anniversary
But no more wishes are worth asking for,
When everything is falling apart 'tween us

I miss listening to the music of my homeland
Where I see myself as lucky or even a loser
I'm a happy being dancing by the flowers
Stepping on the leaves that will hide my grave

I just want to go back and fix the damages
I tried to fold my mistakes from the past
While love letters and roses bloom under the rain
But you ignore my tears and miserable smile

My grandma died before Mother's day
She's away and unseen, unheard, and unsure
If she will understand the reason why is her
Veil is now worn by the moon in the early dawn

Nobody wants to remember me anymore
Nobody cares if I will live for today or not
So many pictures taken and familiar faces,
Unfortunately, those faces are no longer the same

I'm sorry for being who I am to you all
Maybe I should let my heart break slowly to
Feel the distance between life and death
The veil of the moon is my grandma's face waiting on me

Ahmad Al-Khatat

Blood and Ashes

They will burn my flesh
Stop me from having
Breakfast with a Buddha

Justice is no longer true
The judge said I'm sorry
But your worth blood and ashes

The fisherman catches no
Fishes but waves of a salty
Sea that he believes he'll get

The pastor dreams about
Touching the face of Jesus
And ignores my heavy rain

I destroyed my bright side
Love waves to my attention
As death takes a ride home

I'd feel lost in between the
Shade and shadow, till I fall
Dead on earth and not in paradise

The promise of an angel
My last breath was the size
Of cities, my words were the unknown island

There's more than one way
Home, and Baghdad doesn't
Love as much as I thought 'fore.

I Am the Water...

I am the water that gives
the seeds in exile a birth
with inspiration and love

But in Baghdad I'm a tear
of a street that is filled with
Dead crops and red blood

Or a drop of rain that
Rises the devil and
lets two brothers fight

Until I will be a stranger
in other countries and
not a son of my homeland

My kindness is enough for
a homeless to dream about
a neat and warm little house

Ahmad Al-Khatat

We Are Lost

We are lost without boundaries
We want to see ourselves as cool
We forget that we are growing up

Young boys walk with full makeup on
Young girls dance without clothes
Young kids get lost in what to choose

It's funny, we are fearless to pain
It's miserable, we will die fearfully
It's confusing, we judge by skin color

The sun rises and wishes not to set
For observing the blooming roses
For hearing the birds tweet all the way

Yet humans wish to be a clueless
Drink till he can't find his way home
Eat till he can't fit positive knowledge

Smart phones are the new smart bible
We read drama and play with the devil
Ignoring the hungry kids on the street

Facebook steals our personal stories
And Instagram shares our private tales
YouTube teaches us better then teachers

Gas Chamber

Today dogs talk about our idiocy
They don't bark like my boss does
Whenever I try to do something good

Although some of us have to enjoy life
And fold over those headache matters
Just be always bliss and optimistic for

Nobody but your own self or own will
Remember that you have a heart to
Love one and not to please ten faces

Ahmad Al-Khatat

Tears Fall from My Eyes

As tears roll down my cheeks
The moon hides behind my grief
No more fairy tales I will hear
My grandma passed far away

In the midst of most depressing
Winter and here I am weeping
Next to a table by the window
Smoking my sorrows inside out

My heart is painfully aching and
Burning like a candle in the dark
When I slaughtered death and
My grandma innocently died

I can't even believe that she's not
Here, I am sorry grandma I was just
The stranger nephew you sadly have
Yet, your death is a broken memory

I wish if I could speak the language
Of spirits to bring you once in a while
To my mother because I hate hearing
My mother moaning about missing you

Grandma don't be afraid of the darkness
In your grave, the white doves from my faith
Will enlighten your coffin with my prayers
They won't sing but they will plant mercies

Gas Chamber

Now that you are buried under my will
Don't judge the spirits with dust just find
The man you loved and married in years
He truly missed you I can tell from the rose

Ahmad Al-Khatat

I Yearn for You

Feel me and observe my darkness
I am melting in a cup of real sorrows
My face is moist like a leaf below
The drops of rain that hold your heart

I am so weak without your warm hands
You promised to never let me go back
To the old pictures by myself in tears
Colour my mouth with their memories

I feel your spirit trying to convince me
To go sleep early and not drink more
New wounds will never heal my cuts
Without you, my blood is cheap wine

Every moment I die more than once
Like a bullet that hits the soldier's helmet
The wind blows all the flowers and roses
That have the scent on every inch of you

I cannot live without you anymore
I am the sea yearning for the salt
I cannot breath without you
I am the soil missing the seeds of you

Ask the strangers in the early morning
And they will tell you that I am drunk as
Long as you are away from the house
We built to keep ourselves together

Gas Chamber

A Dark Soul in a Healthy Church

The blood colour represent the
Meaning of red cross and red power
But I have always seen it as the
Blood of warriors of one revolution

Except in church and the holy bible
It described as the fears and forgiveness
That makes my heart a cold stone
In which I see Jesus as the lord of terror

My pastor has eaten a wireless radio
That would talk about what the body recalls
And never what the mind remembers
In which I have became an atheist mindless

I met with many people but I didn't
Find the rose in their heart instead I feel
The thorn from the way they pretend that
They want me to have an excellent holiday

Christmas is on the edge of the thin
Moon and cold snowing weather
Yet, I was looking forward to meet with
The loved ones from the church I used to go

I was never alone with tears falling down
I unlocked my spirit when darkness is my
Only friend and if I die for nobody but I would
Break my heart into cents of a smiley homeless

Ahmad Al-Khatat

Lots of lower class families donated money
To the charity of healing school tomorrow
Even though I heard sorrowful whispering from
The characters shadows from the church window

I spoke kindly to the wife of my new pastor
After we danced together on the blessing water
That I need some money to visit my sick mother
Before she dies from calling my name hopelessly

She and I were been through the lost souls
She owned a husband who love God so much
That he sleeps with the unknown nuns from
Different churches so his wife slept with me instead

She loved me and managed to steal the money
Of the charity in church and give it to me the whole
Amount and minutes after I heard that she died
From drinking dozens of bottles of hard liquors

Between the bright day and dark night I arrived
Back home to my small town and once I reached
To the clinic on the Christmas Eve I met with my
Mother laying on the bed dead with dried eyes

The money that I have stolen from the church charity
They were only enough to pay the last days that my
Mom spent alone in this dirty clinic but I was shocked
When I knew that the pastor of my Sunday's church

<u>Gas Chamber</u>

Have had paid everything and have made this charity
To help my sick mother to get well to surprise me with a
Visit to see me weak and walk with me to a different side
Of the world so I won't be a dark soul in a healthy church

Now I feel that I am the traitor who can't make a promise
I walked outside the clinic and I lit all the money on fire
It looked like a red tent that would never makes my life
Any better my tears and regrets are the dust of my misery

Ahmad Al-Khatat

The Demon of My Religion

The day I was born to life
I somehow died after my
Mother died, in which my
Father was the only person
I knew for the longest time

In my house we have never
Had anything that shows
Faces of other people or
Images from the worldwide
Or even a priceless radio

I only remembered the
Symbols of my religion
And the holy books on
The library shelves with
Two pictures of my mom

My father was the only one
He was allowed to leave the
House with the keys of the
Locked windows in his pant
And so we never had a guest

It was almost like a hospital
With four white colored walls
To all rooms and even wash-
Room but my father was never
Happy but an extreme believer

Gas Chamber

We never celebrated a holiday
I was mainly the unlucky daughter
He said to me on my birthday
Whenever he comes back home
With empty hands but very drunk

The day I noticed that my breasts
Are bigger than before I asked him
For a new bra he laughed like an idiot
And said that now I'm set to be his
Pleasure and forced me to wear my

Mother dress so many times 'fore
He went to sleep and after reading
A few chapters from the holy book
He undressed me and raped me till
He sees my blood on the blanket

I was a grown up woman and also
Clueless about how disgusting when
He kissed me and hurt me so much
Like if I was just a doll due to his
Lusty but I wept when he cried too

I wanted to leave the house but
He punished me so harshly and
Aggressive to the point I started
Not recognizing the morning but
I recognized the dawn from his face

Ahmad Al-Khatat

I always felt like a sad song that
Nobody would sing it but I could
From my daily nightmares with a
Believer and a father of nobody
But to my innocent powerless self

In this brutal and unseen universe
I made a vow to go out and meet
With someone who delivered the
Flowers for every day of the year
To the house from my mom prepaid

He knocked the doors miserably
Cause years and years and nobody
Opened the door to say thank you
Or even smile or touch someone
Else or even feel like a little wife

One day my father left home and
Forgot to locked the doors of the
House and the same florist man
Came with a bouquet of flowers
I saw him after I opened the doors

Sadly, my father saw him and he
Wanted to turned my first joy into
A lot of tears and loneliness candle
She melt down and I wished to die
For knowing that I will be raped again

<u>Gas Chamber</u>

I realized that my father was getting old
He started forgetting the doors unlocked
I secretly started talking and meeting with
The man who looked like a angel from heaven
He taught me lots of things that I didn't knew

I started being more aware of decisions and
Know that my father was more of a sinner and
Not a good believer as he pretended all those
Years alone and kinda started having emotions
And feelings for this man and so we did kissed

The day that my heart broke in pieces of tears
When this man broke the home doors and shoot
My father to death with no words or conversation
Why did he do that especially my father was dying
Of cancer and he gets a few days to live with me

I was shocked to watch the demon of my religion
It's dead on the floor and got killed by the man I
Adored to the point I drew my dreams of his heart
I fearlessly pushed him and asked why my father
He responded because he damaged the angel in you

We cried and I ran to the kitchen and grabbed a
Knife to stabbed myself with no thoughts and I
For once felt the death that my mom and dad
Went through and I saw the killer crying with a
Ring for me to be his fiancée and wife forever

Ahmad Al-Khatat

I Witnessed My Death...

Before I was yours, before
I vanished in the morning mist
I knew that I will be a guest
Between your endless fantasies
While I have you as a painful song

In this world nobody is bliss
Some are dead in the mute graves
Others are alive and dead without a tombs
Some are happy to be the joker in cirque
Others are happy to live on the bare street

I witnessed my death alone
I watched my tears falling down
Surrounding my thick blood dropping out
As if I was a fall cloud dropping frozen rain
So many masks were on during my funeral

If I close my eyes and see you
I will love to taste your buttery lips
And realizes that I should be a grateful
To have you in my life and, together
We'll fight against the darkness to be free

Gas Chamber

Ahmad Al-Khatat

Ahmad Al-Khatat was born in Baghdad, Iraq. His work has appeared in print globally and he has poems translated into several languages. He has previously been nominated for the *Best of the Net* awards. He lives in Canada.

colophon

Gas Chamber, by Ahmad Al-Khatat,
was set with Trebuchet MS fonts
by SpiNDec, Port Saint Lucie, Florida.
The jacket and covers were designed by
Kris Haggblom, Port Saint Lucie, Florida.

www.ingramcontent.com/pod-product-compliance
Lightning Source LLC
Chambersburg PA
CBHW030102100526
44591CB00008B/231